wildflower

jessie sienkiewicz

Illustrated by: Amy Sibert
Edited by: Maria Haas

dedication

to all of the sweetest people.
the ones who have encouraged depth and vulnerability.
you know who you are.
from the bottom of my heart,
thank you.

wildflowers.

brave.

seeds

that take root

by direction of the wind,

alone.

they hold on- regardless.

storm, sunshine, stomping.

they rise up nonetheless.

through the pavement,

amidst a barren field.

painting the ground gracefully

after a fire in the middle of july.

they find a way.

they are so free.

they are never what anything beckons them to be.

they flourish, in every obscure and broken place.

and remind us of the light that is shown in even the darkest space.

they epitomize a beautiful aspect of who I long to be-

bold, brave, and so very, free.

a lot like who we are all called to be,

you and me.

wild, and free.

wildflower

jessie sienkiewicz

<u>I sing out to You.</u>

I sing out to you:

You are everywhere.

You are a face pressed against the glass of a foreign train,

encompassed and full of wonder.

You are a walk through city park in the fall.

awake before the sun.

You are a cup of coffee on a tuesday morning

after a sleepless monday night.

You are the sunshine sweeping over me-

warming my skin and settling my soul.

You are the first dance at a wedding

where love begins to write its story.

the song you've wrapped up in my heart

that explodes to tell of Your glory.

You are an escape, a get-away, a haven.

You are a friday night spent in solace,

when the world becomes all too much.

You are a late-night drive without a destination,

and an adventure without a compass.

and You sing over me:

you are created- formed and fashioned.

you are sanctioned, before time began.

you are authorized and equipped- for battle and providence.

you are a bouquet of wildflowers,

on display at the corner market.

you are a captivating melody and a contagious rhythm.

you are uncompromised passion.

you are a spark that ignites burning flames.

you are a precious gem on the floor of an untainted river.

you are an open field with no agenda.

you are creativity overflowing through a pen and a notebook,

and beautifully scattered thoughts.

and I sing back:

You are a torn veil, and undone vulnerability.

You are a well from which others can drink,

and a river that never runs dry.

You are raw honesty, and saturated integrity.

You are unrelenting grace,

unfailing love,

and unapologetic joy.

You are a pine tree on a mountain side,

extending peace and contentment.

You are the air in my lungs,

and the reason that I sing.

and once more You sing back:

you are a creator, a dreamer, a leader.

you are brave beyond what you can see.

you are cherished, and endeared.

you are mine, my daughter.

never stop singing to me.

<u>you haven't seen anything, yet.</u>

my dear daughter,

oh, how I love you.

my little wanderer,

with a mind full of wild forests,

and eyes that zealously anticipate voyage-

just like a child.

a heart that desires for My name to be known,

and footprints eager to be painted

all over the world.

come with me, my wanderer,

I have so much more to show you,

so much more in store.

<u>lies disguised.</u>

sometimes I mislay my temper,

or I become all too disposed

to shrivel in tightly

to the perceived certainty

of the lies I have come to consider.

and I lock people out

and throw away the keys.

and usher them away with smiles and

diverted questions and absent eye contact.

somehow, I impression that I am simply not enough.

but other times I overflow wholly.

and whether by beckoning, invitation, or nothing at all,

the dam of my heart breaks and pours forth

everything real and raw and rendering.

where nothing is hidden

and my tears slowly gather

on the edges of my long sleeve t-shirt.

and I quickly apologize when I realize how little I left

locked away.

and suddenly I feel like I am all too much.

and so,

we teeter-totter between these two lies,

giving them turns to be our truths,

for a moment.

<u>soul rest.</u>

maybe your soul is tired

because all it needs is more time

with Truth.

maybe your heart is tired

because it has been fed

with all the wrong things.

run home, dear child.

run home.

july.

you've always kind of been that way,

haven't you?

you've taken the pain in your heart

and you've curated knives that you choose to turn around

and stab others, hoping that maybe they will feel

like you do.

and you take peoples words,

and you make them your own,

adding poison and profanity as noise leaves your lips.

you'll tell people you love them,

but exploitation is your lifeline-

using any vulnerability they handed over to you as a weapon

for their demise.

but you wear a crown of innocence,

and you point the finger elsewhere.

because you've been hurt before,

and life hasn't been easy for you.

this you never let people forget.

you've been dealt a tough hand,

but refuse any that reach down to pull you

out of the dark.

because there you've found a home-

and you thrive on hate and dragging people

downwards towards where

you wish they were.

you've had a hard time,

with life and love and happiness.

and for that, hearts are broken-

a kamikaze effect.

but please tell me this-

how long must you weave your webs of deceit and cruelty

until you realize you've strangled all of those who ever tried

to break through

and save you?

<u>a good Father.</u>

I see a loving Father,

and a darling girl,

playing on the playground,

and the weather looks just like her-

warm and welcoming and full of promise.

and her blonde pig tails match her bravery

as they paint a story of her innocent messy.

she reaches for the monkey bars,

and He lifts her up so high,

so that she can touch them,

and hang there on her own.

she runs towards the slide,

and reaches out her hand,

and He grabs it,

and guides her down, so gently.

she jumps onto the swing,

and beckons His hand,

to push her high enough,

to touch the sky.

and He smiles at her wonder

as she grasps for the clouds.

she jumps off.

and as she runs,

I see her fall,

and I saw the tears that welled up

in her eyes.

but her Father comes running,

and gently kneels near.

He dusts her off,

kisses her scrapped knee,

and embraces her.

she looks up at Him,

and smiles wide.

He lifts her up onto

His shoulders,

and they make their way back

home.

<u>choose wisely.</u>

the decisions you make

affect more than just you.

am I the first to tell you

that they affect me,

too?

heaven knows.

since when did creativity

convey immaturity?

and when did individuality

marry uncertainty?

why has imagination

become so hushed?

and why has childhood

felt so rushed?

why did dreaming

pack up and move away?

and why did comfort

come and replace its stay?

who told despair

that it has authority here?

and who told adventure

to safely stay near?

where is wonder,

and to where did it leave?

where is laughter-

what made it cease?

why does my heart

feel tied down with a rope,

the moment it departs

to tell of a hope?

it comes quickly back down,

and hits hard the floor,

until it, too, agrees

that we are to dream no more.

yet my soul knows this is simply not

what I was created for.

take me home,

take me home.

Heaven knows

I was created for

more.

to dream of Home.

I have always been one to only show up where

I know I am welcome,

to show up where

I know the bullets won't pierce.

where preparation can be my blanket of comfort,

dangling over my shoulders with a whisper of acceptance,

and assurance.

where I know no one will ask me to be more of myself,

no one will be able to step inside and

touch all of the pieces that I have stretched caution tape around-

all of the neglected and left behind and forgotten and feeble wounds.

honestly, I am so afraid of walking in somewhere and

being known,

fully and really and truthfully known,

all before I have had the chance to

hide my yesterdays and dry my tears.

and put on my bravery

like my blue rain boots that have never been damp.

I am afraid I will show up somewhere and

people will see me for what I feel sometimes;

left behind, messy, afraid, insecure, unsure, shaky,

hidden.

everything that keeps me from sitting safely

and neatly inside of the world that everyone else seems to do so

effortlessly.

a world that doesn't feel at all that homey,

to me.

but then again, this isn't home,

is it?

some days, that reminder makes all the difference-

a truth that comforts through the night.

this isn't home,

after all.

my dearest sister.

laying on the pavement today,

starring up at the billowing clouds

reminiscent.

thankful.

growing up and growing old

always seemed so far away.

who would we marry,

where would we end up,

were questions that fell feeble

to the pebbles between our toes

and the wander in our hearts,

and the summer sun that always brought out

the freckles on your nose.

our messy-headed pig tails

and sleepy eyes

that reflected our wonder and awe

to wake up each day,

and just be alive.

the moments I will never forget

marked only by the smiles,

the scrapes on our knees,

and all that we would grow to learn

and to love.

thankful.

for the swing-sets in the sunsets

of the spring nights that we swore would last

forever.

and we would chase the ice cream truck

and play dress up

and pretend that our bikes were horses.

thankful.

for the pinky promises,

that we would only ever fall in love with dad,

and we would only ever hold hands with each other.

thankful.

for a beautiful mother, and a loving father,

and a loyal army of siblings.

and for that little house on prince street,

that wrote the entire story.

from the day

you became my big sister,

until this moment as I reminisce,

right now.

thankful.

you're the keeper of all my secrets,

the one I know will never judge.

you're the friend that everyone needs

the rare one that few can actually be.

you're a heart of purity

that I can't help but go to bat for

the innocent, childlike giggle

that can pick any heart up off the floor.

the gentle, sound wisdom

that sets my feet on solid ground.

you're the beckoning, gentle love

that welcomes the lost to come home,

and be found.

the sun breaks through the clouds,

and once again reveals the sky of blue,

and as I stand up to walk inside,

I can't help but believe that

everyone deserves a sister like you.

<u>too close for comfort.</u>

you call to me with every step

drawing my eyes to you.

stealing the serenity of the here and now.

you've always done that,

haven't you?

swiftly taking me into your trap

tainting and changing

the trajectory of my vision

from the hope of the horizon

to the unsteadiness of the pavement.

until all I see is the

cracked and the coerced and the channeled.

the inward turmoil and torture

of the projection of all my flaws

on the faces of every passerby.

and you whisper in my ear

with every walking step.

etching tally marks on my heart

of my failures and fallings.

and you convince me

that everyone already knows.

or that, if they did,

they would turn and walk away.

I drop my head in shame,

and you ask for my hands

to shackle them to yours.

you've recorded the judgment

and planted the tape in my mind.

I've memorized every line.

but I must warn you,

there is Truth in the making

and it's sinking deep

and it's taking over

with purification and removal

of all you've woven and bound,

dear approval.

<u>I have.</u>

have you ever met someone

who encompasses an

undeniable affinity for living?

one that can swiftly, yet gently

draw you in,

and take your breath away

all at once?

who has a voice

that echoes off every crack

and crevasse of your heart,

and calms

every storm of your soul?

and whose eyes embody

truth unrelenting?

whose bare feet have set themselves

on soil around this spinning,

swaying world,

and whose scars paint a picture

of every story along the way?

whose fingers dance

with the movement of a rhythm,

and whose mind can take

a mess,

and turn it into a

miraculous melody?

whose smile is

reassuring,

yet evokes a wonder

to grow and to learn, more?

and whose touch steals

every trace of your attention?

whose soul is in full pursuit

of the Creator's,

and whose heart is

all too susceptible

to steal your own?

<u>the pain of an exhale.</u>

do you ever feel like you're just waiting?

waiting to get home,

close the door,

fall into bed,

and breathe again?

sink under a blanket,

and let everything go,

that you've kept buried inside

all day?

the moment that provides relief,

yet evokes desperation?

and you realize how tired you are-

how tired you have been.

you begin to realize how many people

don't really know you.

the pain and hurt that you've worked hard

to conceal

suddenly catches up to you.

tears break the surface,

and remind you to blink.

<u>to step out of the shadow.</u>

but I was always told to be something less,

or something more,

or something other than

who I was before.

as if my character beckoned critics to my door.

and isn't it ironic?

how our truest selves have been shunned

and replaced with mere replicas that look eerily similar

to the person next door?

and so on, and so forth,

until individuality is replaced with confidentiality

and uncertainty

and an accentuated aroma of

aristocracy.

and I guess I've always felt a little drawn into

authenticity

and a heart that beats with passion

on the floor.

a heart that doesn't really mind who comes

to the door,

because it doesn't hide and hinder.

it wants to know more,

to see what's in store,

of the heartbeat

of the one that longs to soar,

anyway.

distant relatives.

do you think about me?

I think about you.

or at least,

I used to.

I don't as much,

anymore.

a heart can only break

so many times,

over the same thing,

until it lets go,

of hope for anything more.

I never heard great things

about you,

but I guess I still

hoped

for arms stretched open wide,

an apology for the past,

and a promise for the future.

I always figured you would want that,

too.

I am all grown up now.

but then again,

you didn't care

when I was just a little girl

with pig-tailed blonde hair.

I needed you then,

but you were never there.

a piece of me

still cries out,

and aches.

do you think about me?

I guess I do

still think about you.

<u>I have a tendency</u>

I don't know about you,

but I have a tendency to run.

I have a tendency to hide.

I have a tendency to brush tears aside,

and tell myself, " toughen up, you're fine."

I have a tendency to conceal;

to build up walls.

I have a tendency to fly-

often, and far away.

<u>the Creator says so</u>

I won't apologize

for letting my mind take flight.

it tends to do

just that.

as if it just knew

from the beginning

Who fastened every cell.

it has always known

that there is much more for us

than that which could ever

meet the eye-

far more than what this world

could ever satisfy.

no, I will never apologize,

for I was made for this.

to wonder, to dream,

to bask in untainted bliss.

and no, I will not listen

to the poison overflowing

from the mouths of those

who never allowed themselves

to dream.

I can promise you this-

my mind is a beautiful mess.

full of child-like wonder,

and hope, and dreams,

unanswered questions,

and contentment, there.

no, I won't apologize.

I am cherished and chosen,

and my thoughts from above,

even more so.

the Creator of the universe

even says so.

<u>looking back</u>

nostalgia has a way of

buttering up

the past,

and battering down

the present.

<u>speak up</u>

please

do not be afraid

to speak up.

do not trade in truth for

comfort,

or convenience,

or simply for the avoidance

of a potentially awkward

conversation.

do not trade in the truth for

compliance,

or safety,

or simply because you would rather be

well liked.

do not trade in the truth for

fear,

or complacency,

or laziness;

for popularity or

relatability.

I promise you,

you will not get to Heaven and regret

the times you spoke up

for truth's sake;

for His sake.

I promise.

speak up.

who is the broken one, now?

I know, it is so hard.

his grip was comfortable,

and his heart was familiar.

but darling, he is not home

anymore.

you fought for him,

you forgave him.

it is so beautiful,

how you always choose to see the best in others,

that way.

how you pursue hurting hearts,

and you have eyes to see others

for all that they can be.

it is beautiful.

oh, but darling,

it is so dangerous.

because it does not always turn out so beautifully.

can't you see?

it turned into

falling head over heels in love

with brokenness.

you didn't see his past

dragging behind him,

like chains waiting to imprison you, too.

you didn't see the demons

inhabiting his soul.

you didn't see the dishonesty,

inconsistency,

or deception.

no, you didn't see the stories

never adding up.

of course, you didn't see those things,

how could you have?

your beautiful soul was just loving the person

beyond the broken.

but do you see, now, why it is so terribly dangerous?

because who is the broken one now, darling?

<u>we were made for this.</u>

this life is truly

such a gift.

our souls long for

adventure,

freedom,

and mystery.

our lungs long

for fresh air,

and our feet long

to leave trails along

every mountainside.

our hearts long to unveil

the love story that has

already been written for us.

I breathe this in,

and breathe this out,

and I hear my Father whisper,

run free, my wanderer,

run free.

and I find myself in awe

again,

as I still cannot believe,

that this life was

sacrificed,

curated,

and created

for me.

a life restrained.

my curiosity

is like a caged bird.

only free to explore

in safety.

but birds don't fly

with caution,

and caged birds

still yearn

for more.

and don't the mountains

call for us?

and doesn't the sand

make for a soft place

to rest your head?

and doesn't the night sky

tell the most sanctifying

bedtime story?

my soul connects best with

what I tend to deprive it from,

the most.

but tell me then,

if birds travel,

why do I chose to cage myself?

for am I not more than a bird?

what a complex contradiction-

to know the freedom of a bird,

yet to not leave the cage,

and fly.

shallow places.

she planted her roots

in shallow places,

and wondered why

a drizzle

felt like a

hurricane.

stop running.

breathe out expectation,

breathe in authenticity.

the you at your core,

longs to shine through.

and aren't you exhausted?

trying to be someone

you're not?

how long must you run?

and pretend?

until your knees buckle beneath you

from the weight of the truth

trying to shine through the facade?

let go. hit your knees.

sometimes it takes just that,

to remind you

maybe you don't want to run the race,

that everyone else is running.

and maybe you're tired

of trying to blend in.

dear.

your mind is far too beautiful

to be filled with doubt and fear.

you have gone through too much,

and have come out on the other end too many times

to believe that I won't turn this around for good.

you are far too immersed in My promises

to believe lies.

you have experienced My strength too many times

in the valleys of darkness

to foolishly believe that heartbreak

is all there is.

you are far too strong to

hang your head,

and wear defeat like a scarf,

beckoning to look downward,

instead.

you are too familiar with My truth to

let this negativity

consume you.

I wish I could tell you that

the world will always be

pure and true to you,

and that everything will always make

perfect sense.

but I have prepared a Heavenly place for you,

and this world is not the pinnacle.

I never promised an easy life,

and I know that this is hard.

but please fight.

fight through the pain,

the sorrows,

and the uncertainty.

I am fighting for you,

and I will never stop.

thick skin.

take the mask off.

what are you hiding?

and who are you hiding from?

be real with others

and yourself.

stop pretending.

stop sugarcoating your feelings and the truth.

stop compromising your heart cries and your voice.

take a deep breath, peel off the mask, and face yourself.

face the pain you've shoved into the closet of your mind.

face the terror and the fears that have hidden themselves

in between each resounding beat of your all-too-still heart.

face the temptation, and the tension.

look yourself in the mirror and vow to end the familiar battle

within yourself that has consumed you

for far too long.

take the mask off,

and replace it with a contagious peace that declares:

I know who I am,

and I may not have all the answers,

but I've fallen into the arms of the One who does.

and if anyone wants to judge me,

they can take that up with my Creator.

because I am at peace,

and no longer a slave to what you may say to me,

or a victim to what you may think about me.

I am His, and He is so proud.

you can't take that away from me.

here's my mask- I no longer need to hide.

<u>grace anyways.</u>

maybe the bravest thing you'll do today is

get out of bed and

step into every inch of yourself.

and that's okay.

because that's really a brave thing to do,

in a world like this one is.

given freely.

are you pursuing

restoration and redemption

in your relationships?

or do you hold tightly

to the wrongs committed against you,

out of revenge,

in hopes to control

the one who hurt you?

stringing along the

mistakes they have made,

inflicting shame and condemnation,

withholding grace,

as you hope that this very

manipulation will change their hearts,

somehow?

if so, then tell me this,

if God can forgive you

for everything,

who do you think you are?

to withhold this same forgiveness,

from one of His children?

are you, perhaps,

more powerful than

the Creator of the universe?

tell me,

are you pursuing

restoration and redemption

in your relationships?

someday.

maybe someday,

I will stop searching for your face

everywhere I go.

maybe someday,

I will laugh with more than the intention

that maybe you'll see me,

or maybe you'll hear me,

and remember why you fell in love with me,

so long ago.

maybe someday,

I won't long to hear your voice

say my name,

or to feel your fingers

trace my arm.

maybe someday,

every song won't remind me of you.

maybe someday,

I will let go of the hope that

maybe you'll change,

and we will love again.

maybe someday,

I'll move on.

but what if my someday

never comes?

<u>dance with me.</u>

beloved,

you know Me, and you have My heart.

I have loved you so much

that I set you apart.

grab my hand,

I want to dance with you.

I will protect you

and cherish you,

always.

did you know I love your smile?

it makes Me smile, too.

did you know I love your laugh?

it makes Me laugh, too.

did you know I see those tears?

it grieves My heart, too.

you feel lost and lonely,

but you are found and called by name.

I see you when you feel that no one else does.

I hear your voice, beloved.

stay far away from fear.

that is not what I have created.

here, take my love instead.

let it overcome you.

you were made for this.

give Me your sadness, and

every burden.

I can carry it all.

pressures off, beloved.

dance with Me.

<u>homesick for heaven.</u>

it is possible to love

where you are,

yet long

for where you come from.

to be invested

in the here

and the now,

and, yet,

to be homesick

for Heaven.

<u>beauty from ashes.</u>

I've always had a special affinity for things of old

being restored to things of new.

from weathered furniture to a shattered heart

and every detail in between.

those things- those people- those parts of you-

that have been battered and broken and left behind,

because something better came to replace it.

but I long to see the bruised brought back to breathtaking.

to be given life again, like two old lovers having the

how'd I let you get away? conversation,

as an aroma of new perspective and commonality and curiosity takes over,

all over again.

or like that chair in the parking lot of a corner store that one thought was trash,

only to be brushed off and brought back and used to rock a sweet child to sleep,

every single night.

or like how Jesus found me-

dead and defeated and dwindling in what I thought was delight.

like how He took me and he dusted me off and He taught me how

I was always supposed to sparkle and shine,

when I had only ever known suppression and scars.

I think Jesus has a special affinity for things of old becoming things of new.

for the wreckage to be resurrected,

and the inherent potential to break through,

just as promised.

of innocent endeavors.

as a child,

I used to pick dandelions,

everywhere I went.

I would bundle them up as a bouquet,

and give them away.

I didn't see them as worthless weeds,

as the world told me they were.

I saw them as vibrant,

beautiful,

and captivating.

this innocence-

I long to maintain

to see things for what they are,

and not what they're

supposed to be.

the one that sees beauty,

where others see flaws.

how different would our world look if

we saw each other this way,

too?

magenta.

his gentleness contrasts

her passionate personality.

they have different dreams,

but they are both rooted and grounded

nonetheless.

his kindness has wooed her into knowing

how to be still and truly exhale.

his process through song intrigued her,

and taught her how to love

in a way she didn't know how.

she invited him into an understanding

that, to love the Lord is to love people;

and he taught her that to live life fully is not to be

isolated or smothered.

she taught him how to be content

in the tension of all of it.

he taught her how

to be let go of the burdens

and grab hold of grace.

<u>from hindsight.</u>

it usually ends this way-

covered in scars

from grabbing weapons

that I thought were roses.

from chasing darkness

that I thought

was just shadows.

from drinking poison

that I thought was

a promise.

<u>regardless of darkness.</u>

there are some things

I will never understand.

this surely cannot be the fulfillment

of the way things were planned.

this world is consumed by

corruption,

abduction,

destruction.

our attention is consumed with

success and production.

I don't understand what drives someone to become abusive,

or a government to become obtrusive,

or promising words to become illusive.

I don't understand the commonality of suicide-

how someone can have no one

in whom they can confide.

I don't understand how the pain of one

can steal innocent lives of others

with his own gun.

or how a father and son can go out

to see batman one night,

and only at their funerals with friends and family

reunite.

you see, I don't understand betrayal or divorce;

those who forsake and hurt others

and feel no remorse.

I don't understand senseless murder or careless abortion;

how our actions are driven by mere distortion.

I don't understand how commitment

has become unheard of,

how deception and lust

have become mistaken for love.

how we all walk around with a disguise of happiness on-

how expressing any kind of emotion has become

inherently wrong.

I don't understand beauty through the lens of society.

they tell you to have all of the latest,

a thin waist, and paint on our nails.

but turn around and say, *don't forget that natural beauty*

always prevails.

can you see the hypocrisy?

how gentleness and kindness are trumped by

notoriety?

how immorality and drunkenness is more supported than

faith and sobriety?

how we are told to be ourselves and then condemned for that

variety?

I don't understand how women can be objectified and sold,

or how millions of people must sleep on the streets every night in the cold.

while there are thousands of people drowning in riches and gold.

no, I know this cannot be how things were supposed to unfold.

yet, there is one thing that gives me hope as an anchor for my soul.

that, amid this broken world, is able to keep me whole.

while there is so much in which I do not understand,

every evil of this world does not reside in

God's Promised Land.

striving doesn't sleep.

heart heavy.

spirit dry.

deprived of nutrients,

sleep,

and You.

endlessly exhausted.

dragging my feet.

tears welling up in my eyes.

tired of feeling

misunderstood.

beginning to agree

with the lies.

thinking foolishly,

and speaking death.

as another night sky fell,

I thought,

surely

I have failed You.

<u>too good to be true.</u>

do you remember that one summer?

we would drive around town

in your pick-up truck,

and go to that one restaurant

that we both loved so much?

and we would take the food and drive

to that one spot by the lake,

and we would watch the sun go down?

and we would slow dance

in the parking lot

to that one song,

do you remember it?

you would sing it back to me,

I couldn't dream of going nowhere,

the lyrics still ring in my head,

and I still cringe at the irony,

between those words

and how our story unfolded,

eventually.

<u>to cut ties.</u>

you've come knocking on my door

far too many times,

by now you'd think I'd have the sound

memorized.

and you've been a liar

far too many times,

by now you'd think I would know better.

but still you show up

speaking in rhymes,

reminiscing as if we are old friends.

but I am beginning to see right through

the facade and the falsity and the foe

in your nature.

for every time I have latched on,

from being led on by you are your words,

I always end up lost and lonely and lied to.

and you always come in the night,

bearing comfort and ease and a promise

that tomorrow won't feel so hazy and haltered,

because the harness will be in my hands,

next time.

but it never happens, and I fall again,

feeling more battered and worn

than ever before,

what happened? you swore

this time would be different.

I hear you knocking,

but this time, I'll be locking

the door.

I won't listen to what you have to say

anymore.

it has been a long time coming,

but this is where it ends.

goodbye control,

we were never friends.

<u>take me here.</u>

falling deep into Your heart,

into a state

where the evil one cannot

tear me apart.

arms open wide,

no looking back.

free to see who I am in You,

and not just what I lack.

surrendered is all my doubt

and my fear.

transform me, Lord,

and take me here.

no longer seeking the world's eyes,

for the world is blind,

and consumed with lies.

I am not defeated,

I see You in me.

shackles unchained,

in You I am free.

for freely I've been given,

so now freely I give

the news of this freedom

for all those who live.

I am cherished by You;

You hold me dear.

You know my every thought;

You've counted every tear.

the taunts of the evil one

uprooted,

as your truth overwhelms.

sin washed away,

eyes fixed on heavenly realms.

no longer do I worry,

for I know You are near.

transform me, Lord,

and take me here.

<u>tear-stained reminders.</u>

sometimes memories sneak into my mind

and then through my eyes,

and they roll down my cheeks.

and the heartbreak sets in,

as each tear hits the floor,

reminding me of what's simply not here

anymore.

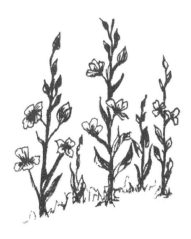

to see myself in her.

I wandered into her room.

her precious, innocent eyes were

tainted red,

and her face

shimmered with tears.

how's my girl? I whispered.

she used the back of her

little, sweaty hand to

simultaneously dry her tears,

and secure her hair behind her ear.

her head dropped.

tonight, had been the winter dance.

she had been overcome with butterflies and excitement,

ever since the boy in her art class had asked her to be his date.

she began to cry again and told me that

he never showed up to the dance.

my heart broke for her.

she looked so beautiful.

my heart broke for her

in so many ways,

and for so many reasons.

I looked down at her, and found myself

desperately wishing

that she was thirteen months old,

instead of thirteen years old.

desperately wishing she was just a baby,

crying because she was tired,

or hungry,

or anything but heartbroken.

desperately wishing I could bundle her up,

hold her close,

and spend forever shielding and protecting her heart.

it had hit me right then-

she would grow to see things I've seen,

hurt in ways I've hurt,

experience things I've experienced.

this pure and lovely soul

will be exposed to a reality

that is devastating,

and corrupt.

a reality fixated on the continual cycle of

pursuing innocence and capturing it,

and destroying it.

my heart breaks for her because

she doesn't see it,

but I do.

she doesn't see the sleepless nights,

the chaos and confusion and tears.

the darkness that crowds too close.

the secrets told and kept from you,

and the days you feel oh, so,

worthless.

she doesn't see the wonder over,

if she left, who would care?

who would chase her?

she doesn't see the betrayals.

leaving her feeling like

there's nowhere to run.

nowhere to run except into the arms

of people she shouldn't be trusting.

falling too far

into dangerous traps.

she doesn't see the nights of feeling

so desperately, alone-

silently breaking beneath the covers

of her bed,

as she cries out.

she doesn't see the constant societal reminders

that you're never good enough.

she doesn't see the friends

that commit suicide,

or drown in addiction.

she doesn't see it,

but I do.

I've lived it.

and so, my heart hopes,

and so, my heart prays,

that her eyes never should see

all that I have.

I would do anything to protect her

from all of that-

to land lock her to her youth.

where swing sets and saturday morning cartoons

were all she looked forward to.

where footsie pajamas and her princess costume

were the only outfits she needed

to conquer the day.

where snow angels, ferris wheels,

and holding dad's hand

were the most cherished of moments.

where her dreams were obtainable,

and her fears were shakable.

I would do anything to take her back there,

and keep her there.

her precious face glanced up at me,

and as I blinked,

our tear drops together

hit hard the floor.

kindred.

line for line,

your story and mine,

aren't the same,

at all.

I don't know you,

you don't know me,

and we will probably

never meet.

yet we can both

look up,

and see the same

moon.

we are somehow

still connected

through the

wind,

and the trees,

the hurt,

and the gravity

that threatens to pull us

all down.

do you feel that, too?

I think you do.

because

I don't know about you,

but I think we are all

a bit more in rhythm

than we care to recognize.

line for line,

your story and

mine.

a hope for tomorrow.

I think you know what I'm talking about-

that stirring in your tummy of all things

raw and real and rendering.

and that stirring in your mind of all things

unseen and undermined and misunderstood.

the impulsive release that you thought was surrender,

only to reel it right back into your own arms.

the feeble grip and uncanny scars that gripe and grind

and drive you into an utter exhaustion.

the pacing and the racing and the wondering and the hoping.

that maybe someday it will be simpler,

a little less stagnant and stuck and a little more still and steady.

and maybe a little less confusing and a little more clear.

a little less hostile and a little more hospitable.

a little less restless and a little more relaxing.

I think you know what I'm talking about.

and it will.

I know you don't see it now,

but it will.

to plant a garden.

I hope you find the one who will

plant flowers in your hair,

and surprise you with coffee,

and take the time to learn every facet of

who you are.

I hope you find the one who will cover you

in nothing but truth and respect,

and do nothing but reflect the heart of the One you belong to.

I hope you find the one who

doesn't tolerate fear or temptation or jealousy,

and I hope he reminds you that you shouldn't,

either.

I hope you find the one that sticks by your side

even when you cannot see the light of day;

who loves you on your best days and your worst days

just the same.

I hope you find the one who is brave and strong and

true to himself,

and calls you out on being anything shy of that

yourself.

I hope you find someone you can be completely undone with,

who looks beyond your teary, red-stained eyes

and believes in your beauty,

still.

and reassures your worth,

still.

I really hope you do.

the change I never chose.

golden leaves

and growing things

that fall and fade

away.

darker nights

and colder days

that come and replace its

stay.

<u>even still.</u>

it had been a week,

in those cold little rooms

of those buildings

that no one wants to be

inside of.

the nurse was new-

she poked me,

so many times.

she couldn't find

a vein.

and I couldn't find

a hope,

that I would ever

be the same.

my hair was

in a knot-

it complimented

my gown,

and my collection

of flimsy,

plastic bracelets.

my mother leaned over

my bed,

and fixed

my oxygen mask.

she whispered,

you look so

beautiful,

and I believed her.

intentional disposition.

I am being trained in the art

of standing my ground.

of wearing my personality

on my sleeve.

of being someone

who enters a room, and

doesn't feel the need to

become any smaller.

but instead just fills the space

as best as I can.

I never excelled at social hour;

small talk is particularly painful for me.

the truth is,

my words fell in love

with paper,

but not

with noise.

I have always gotten frustrated

with the irony of the

effortlessness

of writing a poem,

and the absolute

war zone

of conversation.

I am being trained in the art

of sinking deep

into a Backbone that fills me up.

I am being trained in the art

of realizing that

I never needed to be someone

other than who I already am.

I'm supposed to be like this.

just like this.

it's time.

it's time to forgive yourself

for once accepting less than

what you deserved.

for letting evil into your heart,

for falling for all the deceit

that you thought was different,

this time.

it's time to forgive yourself

for never being able to love

in halves.

for giving yourself to someone

who did not know what to do with

the fragility of your heart,

and the beauty of your soul.

it's time to forgive yourself for hoping-

for having faith in the softness of love,

and how it can prevail.

it's time to forgive yourself

for trying so hard;

for believing so ruthlessly that

I love you meant *I'll stay.*

it's time to forgive yourself

for the people who walked away.

for the ones who didn't fight,

for the ones who made you feel that

you weren't worthy of being loved

the way that you love others.

it's time to forgive yourself

for the way in which you trusted,

as you grieve the fingerprints and memories.

it's time to understand that

you cannot bend someone

into someone who

respects you,

or values you,

or knows you.

trust me when I say that

there is a Love out there

Who understands the very language

that your heart speaks.

and He won't run, or

fumble at the depths of you.

He won't take you for granted.

His love will feel that it was made for you,

just for you.

because it was.

do not let your scars convince you

that your heart does not hold value.

instead, let His scars convince you

that you are loved enough to die for.

<u>no need to pretend.</u>

in this world,

one of the most beautiful things to feel

is someone encouraging you to reveal,

not conceal.

someone actively seeking to

know your heart-

what captivates your mind;

what tears you apart.

someone willfully on a messy, tiresome

chase

to know what lies beyond

the smile on your face.

where you have been,

they too long to be.

what you have seen,

they too long to see.

only then can they understand;

only then can they know,

exactly what is consuming your mind,

without you saying so.

it's an unpronounced soul connection,

in surrendered acceptance

of rejection and failed perfection.

something more beautiful,

I cannot comprehend-

when you're in the presence of another,

and there's no need to

pretend.

<u>open your eyes.</u>

His glory is all around us-

it surrounds.

His beauty is in everything-

it overwhelms.

the cross has defeated-

it overcomes.

His grace is unwavering,

yet undeserved.

His kindness invites us closer.

His pursuit keeps us near.

His promises propel us on.

His love conquers fear.

to where can I run, that His

love won't be?

He is truly all around us,

if only we have eyes to see.

the place that built me.

to anyone else,

it would be a compilation of grass and fences.

a play house and trees.

but to me, it is memories flooding my head and

taking over like a hurricane.

experience cultivates our perception, yes,

but it is so much more than just an open space.

it is my whole life, wrapped up into one place-

a location whose creation marks the exact same year as my own,

as if we were born together, grew together,

and now reminisce together.

it was our playing grounds,

where still only the trees know of our secret hiding spaces.

it was our volleyball court and our putting green,

and where I learned how to pitch a softball.

it was our track to run before nap time,

and our favorite place to eat popsicles before bedtime.

it was where my mother would relentlessly watch us

swing on the same swings,

and slide down the same slides, day after day, year after year.

it was where our dreams of being pirates, spies, and princesses

were not only tangible, but experienced.

it was our favorite camping spot.

it was where we would wildly embrace freedom and imagination,

only broken with dusk and the sound of my father

calling us in for dinner.

it was where we planted watermelon seeds and built snowmen.

where we could eat cherries off trees and mint leaves off bushes.

it is where my five-year-old handprint is engraved in the cement,

and it is where we grew up and found ourselves-

full of imagination, creativity, and

a child-like enchantment that not even time can take away.

it is the place that built me,

and it will forever hold my heart.

<u>desert cries.</u>

here I'll raise my white flag

in surrender of my incessant need

to know all the answers

and have it all figured out.

maybe instead I just need

to love and live,

well.

<u>woven in worry.</u>

give Him what you created-

that worry-woven quilt that you're holding

with sweaty, beaten palms behind your back.

all the fears and wonders

and unknowns of the universe,

that unravel you in uncertainty.

let Him walk you through each little square

of the fabric that you've trusted more than your Father.

let Him convince you why each one is powerless in the face of Purity

staring right back at you.

let Him cut it apart and unravel every strand

until the only thing you can hold onto is His hand.

because that's all you really need.

He will tell you that.

just give Him what you created,

and start creating something better,

with Him.

are you?

are you proud of yourself?

for the scars you've collected

from the hearts you've neglected?

for the promises you've made?

for loving in pieces,

with no strings attached?

encouraging depth in a love

that you knew wouldn't last?

are you proud of yourself,

now?

<u>a doorframe embrace.</u>

when I take time to step away from the busy,

and into the real,

I can find the same theme

ringing true in the walls of my heart.

as my mind recalls those instance in my life in which

someone hurt me,

my heart, just as easily, recalls the very pain I felt

in those moments.

almost like an automatic, well-oiled machine that

I never intentionally fashioned.

redundantly and rudely awakened

by the familiar feelings all over again

when a present event unwillingly triggers a past one.

and suddenly there is closure towards others

where there should be openness,

walls where there should be trust

as seclusion fails to take the place of intended intimacy.

suspicion sinks deep regarding perceptions of intentions,

and quickly takes first-impressions and

replaces them with worst-assumptions.

and just when isolation greets me at the door

and convincingly proposes that it is

intended to live in my home,

there's a tap on my shoulder.

a certain kindness in the eyes of the One

who endured all sin and pain and guilt and shame,

utterly exposed and entirely undeserved.

and He tells me, *they know not what they do.*

and He hugs me, because neither do I.

for if I did know, we wouldn't be here.

about to welcome isolation through the doors of a heart

created for intimacy.

spring showers.

april always brought with it a certain nostalgia

that not even buds and blooms could distract from.

it sweeps over me like the dawning of a days past

as the promises fall though my fingertips like

sand through an hour glass.

I always saw you gently fading into the background

taken aback by the noise of my tattered heart beat

and slowly lifting your fingers from every little pinky promise

that spoke a sweet soliloquy into my messy and broken.

and now I look down at the holes in my orange sweater

worn from the long winter we spent

holding hands and drying tears and braving the cold.

but when the sun came back out, it brought a light

that illuminated every stain and sin and shackle

that winter had left behind, and you decided

that maybe I was all too much to carry into spring.

I just never thought you'd really let me go.

the hope.

in the eyes of innocence,

I see a beauty and a truth

that banishes hate

from every corner

of this world.

<u>until forever ended.</u>

you told me

I was unlike

anyone you'd ever seen.

you told me

you knew when I

was about to cry,

because

my nose would crinkle,

and my lip would quiver.

you told me

you loved my dimples,

and my quirky hair.

you told me

you believed in

me.

you told me

you trusted me

like the steady,

beating rhythm of

your own heart.

you told me

you'd always stay

you told me

we were forever.

until forever

ended.

come with me.

a ship is safe

in its harbor.

but that is not what

it was created for.

you are safe

in isolation.

but that is not what

you were created for.

you were created

to love, and be loved.

you were created for

depth, and exploration.

you were created for

community, and relationship.

none of this is safe,

dear one.

but come with me, anyway,

depart from your harbor.

you'll find exactly what it is

that you were created for.

<u>if I'm honest</u>

would it hurt you

to know

that I actually felt

less lonely

when I didn't know you?

departure dreams.

there is nothing expected of me

here.

there is a freedom to rest;

a freedom to wonder.

thoughts

taking flight

alongside every plane.

adventure beginning here-

dreams of departure

are tangible here.

freedom to leave, escape, run.

filled with stories waiting to be told.

where love stories and awaited reunions so beautifully unfold.

there is comfort in the uncertainty.

memories and moments

unforgettable;

spontaneity and surrender

unbreakable.

take me away,

take me far away from here.

but even in my fondest escape plan,

even unplugged and thousands of feet up,

no matter how far I run,

You are always near.

You are here.

<u>oh, heavy heart.</u>

some say pain is

most prevalently painted

in the words

I miss you,

or in being intertwined

and eternally cloaked

in the longing for

one whom

you cannot have.

some would say it is

in the dissonance of

the disconnect-

between what once was,

and what now is not,

and the loss that clings

to the passing

of time.

some would say it is

in the miscommunication-

between your heart's tender cry,

and the world's callous response.

some would say that pain is

most prevalent

in witnessing

the self-destruction

of an invaluable soul.

of one who saw the light,

but chose the darkness,

still.

oh, heavy heart.

oh, tired prayer.

<u>the quietest cries.</u>

I know I look like I am fine,

but I'm not.

all I want is for you to see

that I'm not.

hug me and remind me it's okay

that I'm not.

<u>through Heaven's gates.</u>

You reached straight down

from heaven,

and I swear I could

see Your arm.

I could feel Your

veins and Your grip-

firm, and promising.

You told me to grab hold,

and so, I reached up,

to meet You.

and I felt You

pull me up,

and out

of everything

that was threatening

to keep me pinned down.

the knowledge of now.

and just like a delicate and purposeful tree,

you cannot carry the weight of two different seasons

simultaneously.

there you'll find a violent and desolate and tiresome struggle

of trying to belong in two hemispheres

at once.

there you'll lose every little bit of joy and wonder

and beauty that each season had intended for you-

a joy and wonder and beauty

that each transition promises to bring.

don't get caught dancing in the in-between.

you'll lose the sight of the prepared and purposed path,

for you.

weather the enchantment and the muse of the season

you are currently planted in.

trust and allow the rhythms of grace to intently carry you

along to the next season in due time.

stay present, stay planted, stay patient, My child.

the turning of seasons will come.

distant disappointment.

so many messages I have typed up that

I have never sent.

so many plans I looked forward to that

somehow always fell through.

I cry to be known, but

hit my own wall every time.

then, run back to the paper and

write in my own rhyme.

it is me who is choosing

against intimacy.

as my heart gasps for the very thing

it was created for.

the running continues until

it asks no more.

<u>under His wings.</u>

there may be shaking,

and swaying,

and heartbreak,

and waiting.

but press in, beloved.

take refuge.

He's staying.

<u>take me deeper.</u>

mercy overwhelming,

grace abundant,

kindness unrelenting,

take me deeper

into Your heart.

as we strive and perform,

the angels are weeping.

for what we don't understand

is how freely given

Your grace is.

how truly selfless

Your heart is.

take me deeper.

<u>misunderstood.</u>

she spoke

in rainbows,

but the world

was color blind.

until I believe.

my foggy and faded never understood

forgiveness.

it always seems too sure and secure.

and I always preferred to flirt instead

with the unstable and unsteady.

utterly unconvinced that pure porcelain

could ever shine through my stained red,

once again.

I thought maybe it was supposed to be like this-

scarred and worn.

and I always had an apology on the tip of my tongue

prepared to agree with the ways you might find fault and failure in me,

as my words would stumble and fall and remind you that maybe

I wasn't what you were hoping I would be.

and I knew it was inevitable

for my past and my permanent

to bleed through my façade,

until I was wearing nothing but a scarlet letter.

but the end of my rope

was only the beginning of Yours-

infinite and intricate and intentional.

and You wrap me up,

and carry me onward

with hope and holiness.

and You speak sweet soliloquies

until I believe.

to leave the prison walls.

my soul flourishes in freedom.

where there is safety and sanity in the surrender.

where the bindings are broken-

of perfections and expectations and insinuations

that always clashed with my contentment.

I have tried to fit into the rain-boots of rules and regulations

and religion,

but my bones always beckoned for barefoot,

instead.

my heart knows its home

and it is not in a harness or halter-

regardless of the pressure it feels to believe so.

I have been chosen to flourish in freedom-

in the fields and in Your fortress.

your detained and restrained longs for this,

too.

if you'd only surrender the shackles and let

Him come close to you.

<u>I want to know hearts.</u>

my mind is flooded,

as I look into your eyes.

for what reason does your heart beat?

for what does it ache?

have you dared to dream of

pursuing your heart's deepest cry?

would you risk looking like a fool for love?

or for your dream?

for the adventure of being alive?

have you reached in, and

touched the center of your own sorrow?

has your heart been slit open

by the pain of life's betrayals?

have you been shriveled or closed from fear of any kind?

can you sit with pain?

how you respond in moments of hurt?

who or what is the source of your joy?

do you dance with the wildness that love tends to evoke?

do you believe unashamedly?

without cautioning yourself to be careful and more realistic?

where do you see beauty?

and where do you find life?

do you stand up or sit down

in the face of failure?

what sustains you, when all else falls away?

can you be alone with yourself?

do you truly like the company you keep?

I want to know your heart.

<u>surrender.</u>

complete surrender

comes with losing

any sort of authority

we thought we had

to worry

about what happens

next.

the coldest christmas.

and for the first time

in a long time,

I don't have a plan.

I don't have a direction.

I am going in circles,

and it feels like

the world is passing me by.

I want to say *hi*

but I don't bat an eye.

suddenly I stop.

maybe I am tired of walking,

but I'm not.

I'm tired of running,

tired of pacing,

tired of racing.

I don't want to play

this game that we are all

playing.

I know that I am searching,

I just don't know what for.

and so, I wait,

but can't you hear me?

I don't want to wait

anymore.

I'm undone; I'm restless.

I want to go home,

but I am not so sure

I know where that is,

anymore.

<u>to new things.</u>

this is the end of me

comparing myself

to everyone and everything

I'm not.

this is the beginning of me

celebrating all that it is

God created in me

and the potential of

all that He knows

I can be.

to wonder; to wander.

born with eternity

stamped on our hearts.

a longing,

a yearning,

a wonder.

our path is slowly unraveled,

but we quickly realize how small we are.

our Creator is a pursuer-

He encoded His existence-

for our minds to simultaneously

wonder,

and our souls to disperse and wander.

seeking to know, and

journeying to find.

there is truth in our existence, and

meaning in the rhythm of our

steadfast, beating hearts.

walking aimlessly,

driven by the passion

deep in our veins.

restlessness overwhelms;

contentment no longer

seems attainable, here.

this is our temporary home,

yet, still, we strive.

our eyes are darting, and

our dreams departing-

flying.

flying back to the One who

orchestrated them;

flying away from the one who

never danced with them.

they long for

life,

breath,

fruition;

but motives don't always align,

and we silence our hearts'

loudest cries.

why do we chain and contain,

what was always meant to be free?

why befriend distraction, and

stray from destiny?

but still our minds wonder,

and still our souls wander.

wonder who we are, and

wander with hope

tied to our ankles-

as identity has become rooted

in what we belong to.

there is a Hand

reaching down,

to guide.

but instead we

are led

by what's inside.

until we fall,

and look up.

our own ways

are lifeless,

but our new nature

calls our name.

hearts latching onto

the heavenly realm,

as the truth of our identity,

breaks through our restlessness,

and gently overwhelms.

we were made for wonder,

and to eventually wander,

Home.

<u>dead to striving.</u>

I was

falling,

but I needed

to stand.

breaking,

but I needed

to compile.

yearning,

but I needed

to conceal.

but now I am

failing,

at the hand of

what I thought

I needed.

<u>seasonal hope.</u>

I know that autumn means

that winter lies ahead.

but if winter comes,

can spring be far behind?

strength in scars.

I used to think that fragile

meant weak.

now I know it assimilates

strength.

for to be fragile means you were

crafted and created

and your pieces,

they were placed,

patiently.

every little crack and crevasse,

has been tended to.

to be fragile means you didn't do it

on your own.

it points to something higher,

something greater,

something at work in you

and through you.

fragile.

a battle that has been fought,

a veil that has been torn,

a promise that has been made.

the reliance upon something other than,

you.

a devout dependency on the return of the

Divine.

the beauty in realizing the little control you do have.

and cleaving to the One

who has it all.

audience of One.

above all else, beloved,

remember Who it is you are living for.

it is not the souls scattered below.

I know you find yourself overwhelmed daily

with opinion. image. sin.

hurtful remarks and broken hearts.

trying too hard to find the right words.

spreading yourself too thin.

fighting battles you just

can't win.

replaying all you've done,

and what's been done to you.

but I'm here to lift your head.

because when all is said and done,

it's You and I, beloved.

audience of One.

a constant tension.

I feel a constant tension-

between who I want to be, and who I am.

a beauty that is humble,

and a beauty desperate to be seen.

a heart crying out for attention,

as if deprived- hopelessly deprived.

there is a little girl inside,

who longs to be desired,

and loved,

and seen.

I feel a constant tension-

between what I know I need,

and how I'd hate to be seen.

what about desperation?

a tension between

my heart pacing, and

my mind racing,

through questions,

timelessly.

most of which,

I would never ask-

do you miss me,

when I'm not around?

do you love

who I am?

am I lovely

in your sight?

am I worthy of

your time?

please, tell me,

I need to know.

because I feel a constant tension.

<u>a trip down memory lane.</u>

flooded with reminiscent thoughts.

nostalgia overwhelms as you recall

mountain-top memories from your past.

regretting opportunities

you've turned down, or the mistakes

you've made.

realizing how much you miss

certain people or places from your past.

reliving the moments

you felt the most alive,

sorting through pictures and piecing together stories.

missing your childhood,

when everything seemed

so, much

easier.

realizing how much older you are now,

time is passing by so fast.

looking back at the moments you felt the weakest,

and you can see how much stronger you are now.

recalling how you've been hurt,

realizing that there are some pains you haven't quite let go of.

witnessing the loyalty of the people

who have stayed by your side, and

appreciating them more than you ever have.

don't rush.

let God in.

let Him heal what needs to be healed,

let Him glorify what needs to be glorified.

let Him reassure any doubts you may have that

somewhere along the way,

He left you.

let Him speak truth over your wounds,

and let Him remind you of the amazing people He gave you

to walk through life with.

don't be afraid to reminisce, beloved.

He is a safe, safe place.

waiting to offer healing and peace.

<u>the tired tapes.</u>

all those people-

they've hurt you, I know.

the lies they've told you-

still sting, I know.

the burdens and heartache,

and let downs and mistakes.

they replay themselves

on your bedroom ceiling

every night.

your head

hits the pillow

and you are reminded

all at once

of all those things

you've tried so hard

to forget.

seasons of steadfast.

do you remember who you were

before the world told you who you should be?

do you remember the curiosity, the anticipation,

the scrapes on your knees?

do you remember the bravery, the certainty,

the steadiness of your heart?

the confidence, the unshaken will?

oh, I remember it all.

I reach for this innocence,

as I walk past a golden tree of fall.

its leaves holding on so tightly,

but slowly growing weary,

of the way of the world,

and the course of the wind

that is trying so hard to

uproot.

similarly to the way of the world

and the course of the wind

that has stolen my childlikeness

from me.

one by one,

the notion of winter plucks

each little leaf from the tree.

holding on so tightly.

but just when the winter

thought surely it had won,

the tree bore new leaves

the moment springtime came.

spring is never too far away.

He is never too far away.

winter may take your leaves,

but it cannot take your roots.

oh, how I see myself here.

now I remember who I was

before the world told me who I should be.

revisiting familiar.

take Me the long way

around your heart.

and don't leave anything out

the details are My delight.

and don't shy away from the chaotic

the lucidity is My heart cry.

and don't try to hide the fragmented.

the bruised is My beckoning.

take me the long way

around you heart.

open the windows of apprehension

and the doors of suspicion

and breathe, again.

autumn.

a beautiful blend of

nostalgia,

blessings, and

potential.

yielding a harvest of seeds sown

throughout this season;

bracing us for colder days to come

in the next.

don't be fooled, dear one.

don't be fooled by pretenses,

or the impeccable exposé.

maybe it seems that

you're missing something,

comparatively.

but behind the filters,

and the followers,

we are all just humans-

running the same race,

tired of the same things,

praying for the next change.

we are all just searching,

for meaning and depth,

and purpose and answers.

don't be fooled by facades,

dear one.

take heart.

the ultimate Judge is one

who cannot be fooled

by any kind of smokescreen.

truth above the noise.

do not listen to them.

hear this:

you were not made for the mundane.

you were not a calamity,

or a mishap or a mistake.

you are designated,

never to be another one

quite like you.

you were created on purpose,

and for a purpose.

you were created for crisp air,

and a belly full of laughter.

you were made for

escapade,

unearthing,

miracle.

you were made for a Love,

that takes everything inoperative in you,

and makes you whole,

again.

<u>to see beyond.</u>

but maybe it doesn't have to be this way

there's more to life than to lodge

in the distrusts and the verdicts and the collapses.

there's life below the roadside

longing to prove its purpose, to you.

and I know, all you've seen is crimson red

and the souvenirs of the *has been*.

but there's a novelty blooming in your veiled

and it's drawing into fruition

all the *can be* that your heart can't see.

there is life beyond the skylines and

the tall buildings and the city lights

that were never meant to hold the

weight of your lengthiest nights.

and I know you've tried

to tear off the blinds and get out of bed

and step one brave foot

beyond the doorframe and

into a world

that has always driven you back down

underneath the pavement.

but maybe it doesn't have to be this way.

maybe it starts in the unidentified

a step without the canopy of understanding

to catch you, just in case.

with nothing to guide you besides

a promising Embrace, just in case.

and a Grace to hold your hand

and a Love to set the pace.

<u>subtle remnants.</u>

some things never leave

a person.

like the smell of the t-shirt

of the one you once

loved.

<u>walk on.</u>

and just as she was about to

turn around and give up,

He clutched her hand and said,

don't miss out on something good,

just because it also might be difficult.

it might be difficult,

but it will also be so, so good.

walk on, dear one.

walk on.

He sees us.

closest to God,

amid the unfamiliar.

in the moments of pure

immersion in His creation.

those moments of exploration,

and depth.

witnessing to the breathtaking mountains

that tower over us,

and the waterfalls

that cascade down

to meet us.

the way the galaxies

were so impeccably orchestrated,

and how every star was individually placed.

closest to God,

amid the beauty of this world.

encompassed by and engrossed in

the peace that accompanies His creation.

left winded in wonder

of how much He must love us

if He looks at all His creation,

from the depths of every ocean,

to the last star in the night sky, and

He says these things are

good and with them,

He is *pleased.*

but then He looks at me,

and He looks at you,

and He says we are,

very good and with the creation of us,

He is *well pleased.*

closest to God,

amid the utter allurement of this planet.

trying to conceptualize that

the Creator of all of this,

thinks we are

even more beautiful,

even more delicate,

even more captivating.

amid this

awe-inspiring,

heart-stirring,

astonishing world,

He sees us.

<u>the ones who planted me</u>

you have always just done the best with what you were given,

which wasn't very much.

you planted five flowers that took root and bloomed up through the concrete, of mendacities and prostrate potentials;

sunshine that was helpless to give you a hand;

beneath the skies that hurried along your childhood.

you never really knew steady. you never really knew gentle.

you only really knew arbitration, and the comfort of *just let it go.*

I can see you both back then- acquitted, and golden.

a vivacity in your eye to learn and grow and see.

an venture and a beauty to unravel, printed softly on your hearts,

swiftly taken by death and the chaos and clamored and coerced.

maybe that is what brought you together,

to show you both the sacredness of surrender

to something higher, something better.

all of the tainted and tangled hurt that you needed healing from,

a beckoning love to lavish itself over every missing puzzle piece.

you weren't given an easy course.

but you took each other's hands and you ran, anyways.

and look now, at the garden you've planted.

and those five little flowers that would have never had a chance, otherwise.

<u>daddy's little solider.</u>

my dear daughter,

I made all of the delicate,

picturesque parts of you.

yes, even the ones

you want to tuck away

and hide.

I made your all-inclusive heart,

and I know what makes it beat

faster, and slower.

I know what makes you wounded,

and what you refuse to let

anyone see.

I know what makes you cry,

and the story behind

every, little tear.

I know what interrupts your heart

the most,

and I know how to comfort you

when you are falling apart.

I know how to make you smile,

I know how to love you,

I know how to be a Daddy

who loves.

so, don't worry about darkness-

don't run from it.

remember, you're carrying My light.

remember, you're Daddy's little solider.

<u>the temporary</u> .

assurances break.

intentions wither.

sin pigments.

people let you down.

this world

is not your home.

stop trying to store

your treasures in

tainted,

toxic,

ticking

things.

ragged righteousness.

He said he would take me as I am

in fact, He said he wanted me.

affected and scorn and all too sick of a world

that told me it could save me.

sick of it indeed but also habituated

to the affirmation and the assurance

and an affinity of adrenaline.

the rush of running around amongst the feeble and fallen and

playing hide and seek with expectation.

but He showed up in my sorrowful.

and didn't tell my worn to first become woven.

He told me He wanted me.

and mostly, it felt revitalizing because at the time

I didn't even want me.

but He picked up my pieces, all my speckled and startled.

He told me of a better way

and of a brighter day

and that I could put my trust

in all that He'd say.

He pocketed my battleground, and offered me solid ground.

He acquired my shame and handed me a new name.

one of beauty and beloved and becoming.

He calmed my clenched and

spoke a melodiousness over my soul.

and I declare

I'll never be the same.

<u>a tired guessing game.</u>

why does my heart drop,

when I hear those words-

can we talk?

anxiety engulfs.

panic sets in.

what could they need?

what did I do wrong?

is there something

I am blind to?

maybe I have become too much,

I've tried so hard not to be.

I keep to myself so that

I won't be seen.

are they going to leave?

uncontainable thoughts;

my focus untamable.

life without relationship

sometimes seems

so, alluring.

I would have no one to

disappoint,

because I know I'll let you down.

it seems I am

so, good at that.

what are they thinking?

I just need one clue.

nothing is worse than

entering the darkness

of a battlefield

with no shield.

undone vulnerability,

while they hold the weapon.

I feel exposed,

and far too known.

but they don't know me,

not at all.

so why do I care so much

about what they could say?

they don't know me,

anyway.

this reminds me why it's best

if they just don't know me.

take time.

take time to get away, dear one.

take time to rest.

take time to grapple with your contemplations.

take time to intentionally affiliate them with Heaven.

take time to compose.

take time to be brutally sincere with yourself.

take time to investigate your heart.

take time to lay your deterrents at Jesus' feet.

take time to challenge the very things holding you back.

take time to sit in the tension.

take time for healing, dear one.

take time.

a soul scattered.

it's a complicated

paradox.

but it's remarkable-

how one country can

wholly break your heart,

yet restore it simultaneously,

and somehow steal a piece along the way.

but all the best places do.

<u>the silver lining.</u>

but the sun always comes back out

I know there are hazes around your heart

and a hurricane immersing your attention

and it appears the rain

has overstayed its welcome.

but hold fast, beloved

don't be so quick to reconcile into the storm

and call it your home.

the sun is your saving

be steadfast, beloved

He's there in the waiting.

a story unread.

I used to be

an open book.

but I am not,

anymore.

the stubbornness of my cover,

and the intricacy of my contents,

were not created for fragile fingertips

and meager minds.

my story has been unraveled before-

opened and taken off the shelf.

my spine has been cradled

by hands that were far too feeble,

and focus that was far too fragmented.

my pages have been scanned through,

but I have yet to be placed into

the hands of one whose

tender attentiveness longs to know more.

who doesn't stumble at the realization that,

sometimes my chapters are cut short.

that sometimes my edges are sharp,

and my conclusions confusing.

I have yet to be placed into

the hands of one who

has the intention to read

from start to finish;

persistently dedicated.

it has taken some time now,

but I no longer ache to be

picked up,

chosen,

and entertained.

I have, instead, found

the utmost of consolation

in my story.

I have found a familiar comfort

for the pages still being written.

no longer do I tremble and worry

that my language isn't beautiful enough,

or that my story is one to be hidden.

I can only pray that someday,

the sentences and paradoxes of my heart

will leave traces of their own ink

on the hearts that yearn

for such comprehension.

I can only pray that someday,

I will no longer be taken out of context,

misunderstood, or

scrabbled with.

I have always had quite the affinity for words,

but I had never met a love quite like I did,

when I began to read my own.

<u>go tell of this love.</u>

tell the ones you love

how much they mean to you.

not out of trepidation of losing them-

instead, tell them with the acquaintance

that the exquisiteness in love

should never be pending.

go tell of this love.

this love has the command to

change perspectives,

unstiffen hearts,

and save lives.

remember when.

remember when

we met?

you lied and said

you were available.

because you wanted to be,

for me.

remember when

you even moved

all the way

across the country,

into my little town?

remember when

we spent the summer

in the moonlight?

I swear,

we never slept.

remember when

you promised

to take me home

with you?

to the ferris wheels,

and the boardwalks,

and the notion of

forever?

remember when

you broke my heart?

I swore I'd never

be the same.

<u>surrounded.</u>

the cross before me

the world behind me

the enemy beneath me

and You beside me.

tell me,

how can I lose?

to reflect truth.

it might take some time,

but you'll get there.

that reflection in the mirror that

mimics and mocks

and tells you that you will never

suffice.

the one that picks apart your pretty

and talks your confidence down to a

callousness that chooses to close its eyes

to the truth.

and I know the lies become conversant

and the lines become indistinct

and you forget what it was like

when you were careless in the face of caution

and you believed in the splendor of this world,

and the bravery of yourself.

and I know you question yourself

in the clothes you wear

and the length of your hair

and the details of your fragile skin.

you stare and compare

but you swear

that you won't strive and starve and lose yourself,

again.

and I know you don't see it now,

but you'll get there.

it takes being fed up with the falsity of society

and criteria for loveliness

and being convinced by the truth of the Creator

and welcoming only His annotation into that reflection

in the mirror.

it might take some time,

but you can get there.

where you will walk with a comprehension

of the beauty you regard

and the origin of the awe-inspiring

echo of Him,

when you look in the mirror.

quick to listen.

listening is a vanishing art form.

an art form

painted in the depths of

the heart of our Father.

revealed as

an unrestrained gift,

birthed from a

purified knowledge of

His canvas

of grace and redemption,

that was fashioned

on our behalf.

an art form where

self-regard and diffidence have

gone far, far away

to a place where they have

no authority.

Jesus is personally evident

in those who listen.

listening is a dying art form.

it has become abused and distorted-

we listen to respond;

to unveil our own painting

instead of listening to understand;

to unveil another's.

<u>you didn't stay.</u>

you planted flowers

in my heart,

but you didn't

stay to

water them.

silly me,

I thought for sure

you'd stay to

water

them.

beckoning of the brave.

you see, I supposed that to become strong,

I must first become callous, and exacting.

I must attest to the world that I need no one before

it will be brave enough to lend me a hand to hold;

before it will realize that I'm too busy building up my own walls

to have time to step into the cross fire of another.

and yet, I heard a sweet, gentle, familiar whisper.

reminding me that all I need to be in this

big, spiny, forbidding world,

is still.

the ground beneath me has been shaky,

and my self-made armor has been pierced,

far too many times.

my hands are sweaty, and bleeding

from gripping onto the sheer brokenness of this world

for dear life.

but His whisper reminds me

that holding out these fragments and offering them up

in a promise of surrender will always be

brave and strong and true.

it's okay.

you don't have to fight or defend

or enter the battle alone.

you can be soft and sensitive to the rhythms of grace

and still be a strong soldier to be reckoned with.

just raise your white flag.

just welcome Him back in.

you're almost home, dear one.

<u>return home.</u>

learning to opportune the waiting.

not in the sense of adopting complacency,

but in the sense of forgoing control.

and what a beautiful feeling it is,

to lose control

and gain yourself,

again.

rest in the secret place.

I dare you to be alone.

I challenge you to dig deep,

and find out who you are.

I challenge you to look

at the face in the mirror, and

love yourself as much as you love other people,

because you love the One

who formed and fastened you.

lonesomeness might come.

but when it does, sit down with it and confront it.

discover where there are gaps in your heart,

and let Dad come in and fix them.

you'll discover just how strong He is.

you'll feel alive and whole again,

here.

<u>eternal mindset.</u>

absorb your previous,

reverie your upcoming,

but live in the contemporary.

don't get worked up about the small stuff.

you'll look back and recognize,

it was all small stuff.

eternal mindset, child.

eternal mindset.

pride for humility.

maybe you've disregarded,

that time is a Trainer,

teaching you of trust and

trampling your tradition.

the way you think things ought to be,

needs to bow down to the foothold of the potentiality

of surrender.

the avenues your thoughts have memorized,

need to yield at the notion that, perhaps,

there is a brighter and truer way.

the reactions and justifications that leap forward

from habit and stronghold,

need to sit silenced and tuned in

to the rhythms of grace and the patterns of love.

your religion and your position and your opinion,

must become trivial and trite and traded in

for the pace and the humility exemplified

in the One who died,

maybe you've forgotten, that He is

the way and the truth and the life.

colors overhead.

no matter who we are or

where we come from,

we can see it

just by simply

looking up.

and isn't it marvelous?

how we are all equally

enthralled?

the sky,

the sunset,

the compilation of colors dancing overhead-

unifying.

that's who our God is-

that His formation inhales the weight

of unity into actuality.

and that is who we are-

unified amongst His creation,

under His wings, and

in His promises.

<u>me too.</u>

one of those winter days that feels a little more like spring.

warm enough for sandals, but not enough to forget your jacket

at home.

just a little too perplexing and capricious.

sometimes, a little bit like how I feel.

a little weary in the ways of the world,

and a little unresolved in the unknown.

not quite choosing a path to pursue

while not really ignoring the options either.

just kind of there. you know?

sort of swaying in the in-between of just

not really knowing.

that kind of day where someone asks you a question,

and a simple answer seems suitable.

even though that's not really you.

you're one for depth and validity and liberty.

but today it doesn't feel that way, does it?

it's like feeling exhausted but knowing there's always more

to be done.

feeling burnt out but not having the means to cut back on anything.

and maybe you feel culpable because you should be content all the time, right?

or at least that's what they tell you.

but today, you're battling.

wedged somewhere in the in-between.

me too.

sometimes that's all you need to hear, right?

that what you feel is customary and okay?

you're human and this world is fallen and this life is

sometimes really hard.

but it's okay, because you're here. and

you're not alone. this too shall pass.

seasonal love.

you were the heat

of the summer,

and the promise

of the fall.

and the callous darkness

of the winter.

but when the spring came,

you didn't come back

the way the flowers

are supposed to.

found again.

still your mercy chanced me;

even still, it chased me down,

turned my sorrows into songs,

and my afflictions into

a relinquished,

shoeless,

triumphant

dance floor.

filled my cup,

I am abundant,

with still more to go around.

I thank you, Jesus,

for pursuing me.

that even in the darkness,

You are found.

Your grace is sufficient,

and through my weakness,

You are strong,

I praise Your faithfulness, oh Lord.

You found me, again.

You always, find me.

a dry surrender.

I became so weary of the in-between,

stomping grounds of footprints like memories

of when I insisted on my own way,

when you really just wanted to carry me.

footprints that never meant to fall so heavy on me.

I became so tired of leaving uncertainty

like mile markers on the road of a story

I seemed to be writing myself.

a story that seemed to lazily fall cyclically.

like autumn leaves swirling to desolate underneath,

I decided to match the harshness of winters breaths.

I decided to barricade my blameless behind unsurpassable

assuredness.

I allowed my tired hands to take the reins and my broken erupted,

fiery pieces leaking out all around.

I became so weak in the loss of direction

as my ample ways turned into a apologetic dirt road beneath my feet.

I became so weary.

but still You met me.

I raised my white flag in the middle of that desert.

and You came and You found me.

<u>the familiar ways.</u>

I am tired.

I'm achy in the ways of the heart,

from shallow things,

from growing pains,

that have never made me any taller.

a walk with Dad.

I'll walk in Your footprints,

even if I blunder and fall.

You'll pick me back up,

and position me up tall.

I'll learn from You,

as You guide the way.

I'll do as You do,

and say as You say.

teach me, Jesus,

tell me Your stories,

how heaven bows down,

to sing of Your glories.

show me how to love,

completely, wholly, undone.

how You love even those

who deny You as Son.

teach me of friendship,

and the rhythms of grace.

I'll walk in Your footsteps,

and fix my eyes on Your face.

the truth about time.

time doesn't heal.

it actually doesn't heal anything.

time itself holds no such supremacy.

don't beat yourself up,

when tears break the surface after several years,

of tilling and toiling and trusting that time

would heal.

it never did.

you still feel as deeply

as you did back then.

and it's not your fault-

folly and fictional advice tends to feel

flawless.

but it's really just familiar.

time doesn't heal anything,

it was never intended to fulfill such a role.

it's just the ticking of a clock and the passing of years.

and maybe in between somewhere,

you've forgotten some of the pain.

but the scars are still sore, when you touch them,

aren't they?

they've been covered, but were never tended to.

and I know you don't want to,

but it's time to reenter and recollect

the hurt and the heartbreak and the haunted.

because time doesn't heal.

but I know Someone who does.

let Him in-

it won't be long until you realize

healing doesn't operate in the

predictable and passing ways.

<u>tired tallies.</u>

I know you wake up every morning and

you reach for bravery,

and instead

you're greeted with failures and less-thans.

your heart is broken and burning

with questions and expectations that were never met.

you wear your failures and fears and frailties like

a worn-out sweater in the middle of november.

and you feel just like it-

not quite blooming, not quite barren.

just unadorned enough to recognize that your marvelous colors

have dimmed from a burning orange to a dull that

unwittingly accentuates your serrated edges.

I know you go to sleep each night like

aligning tired tallies on a paper.

promising the world that you make more mistakes

than you're worth.

rewriting tomorrow's script because

you need to become less.

mostly because today you were far too much.

I know your hope has become tattered and

you're wondering if it's all worth it.

but what if, it is?

what if your story is on the brink

of being the very narrative that will save

someone else?

what if this next chapter will be the bridge

that pulls you out of these trenches and

invites you into the sunlight?

maybe this part looks different than you thought it would,

but maybe it was never yours to plan or hold together,

to begin with.

maybe it's time to put the pencil down and

remind your heart,

again,

Who the Author is.

<u>from a distance.</u>

she loved the ocean,

just like she loved him-

she saw the vastness,

the beauty,

the mystery,

and it drew her in.

she loved the ocean,

just like she loved him-

from afar.

far too afraid,

to actually jump in.

<u>tell me.</u>

how is it that you can feel

that you are

too much,

yet

not enough

all at once?

<u>life to death</u>

labels.

a hurtful means of someone

attempting to give you a new name.

a summary of a heart and life in one,

restrictive box.

a box that doesn't inspire

progression or love,

but instead beckons

regression, and demise.

demise where there could have been

existence.

labels.

single words spoken out

that allocate anguish to

shadow us.

we love the one who spoke and

so, we harmonize

with the lies.

we peg them to our hearts.

and so, we implement

our newest identity.

word curses.

death and life reside

in the power of the tongue,

and I think we too often undervalue

the sheer demolition

that our words can have on another heart.

labels.

watch what you speak out over someone.

you can plant flowers

in their soul,

or turn fertile soil

into sterile grounds.

the only One.

I know you're examining.

your heart aches for something,

you just don't know what for.

my prayer is that you'll look up,

and understand there is something more.

my prayer is that at the heart of

wherever you're searching for,

you'll find Jesus there.

for I know the only one who can

justly placate the human heart,

is the very One who crafted it.

<u>from my heart to yours.</u>

do you get down, God?

by the way we have destroyed

ourselves, and

this world?

I can't conceive.

having my pride and joy,

my masterpiece,

look back at me and

tear itself down.

the agony, the anguish,

you must feel.

do you get angry, God?

at the way this has all unfolded,

when your heart was only ever

for completed accord and love?

I can't imagine

opening my entire heart and home

to loved ones, nonetheless,

only to have them hurt each other,

and fight over who gets more.

do you get jealous, God?

by the means of self-medication,

and the realization that

distractions have only multiplied?

I can't imagine

giving my children heartfelt,

good gifts.

only for those gifts

to replace their desire for me.

reminders in the rough.

but you weren't made for the easy things.

your heart beats for battle

and the buoyancy of victory.

I know you fear your jagged edges

are too sharp to enter in,

I know they have you convinced that

you always be damaged and battered.

they sting and scrape and scar

and tell you that you aren't worth the war, at all.

I know it's difficult but

you weren't made for the easy things.

and I know the fight is frightening.

but you are fully equipped,

with swords and shields and grace

that tackle all of the darkness that threatens to overtake.

you are protected before you,

and behind you,

and on every side of you.

your jagged edges aren't weaknesses,

just reminders that you cannot battle alone,

and that you'll never have to.

my solidified confidence.

who am I?

as the world tosses and turns my soul,

and distinctiveness escapes with the spiraling of the seasons,

there You interrupt.

You reach down, touch my heart,

and once again,

You remind me of who I am,

because of who You are.

You remind me that I am who

You say I am,

and nothing less.

You urge me on to walk in confidence,

and to trust You to always come along,

and answer my question:

who am I?

<u>You and You alone.</u>

my one desire.

continue to move me,

continue to tremble me,

continue to contest me,

continue to be fluent to me.

until my heart covets for nothing

but You and Your love,

You and Your heart for me,

You and Your truth,

You and Your plan for me.

<u>He knows.</u>

He knows about every dream you have-

even the nightmares.

He knows why you paint;

why you write.

He knows why you are so hesitant

to clasp true nonconformity.

He knows your entire childhood-

every inside joke.

He knows about your first heartbreak.

He knows about your dad,

and your brothers,

and all their hushed dreams.

He knows every falsehood you fight; every fear.

He knows everything you want from this life,

and every hope and prayer that has ever departed from

your heart.

He knows why your favorite city is your favorite city,

and how you still don't believe that

you are lovely,

and treasurable, and identified.

He knows every little detail.

<u>unified in unique.</u>

I see that you want to be different

your soul thumps for valor and a

earnest, noiseless desire to stand out

in the multitudes,

of others with faces and facades and fire inside them,

that seems unnervingly similar to that which you call,

yours.

you pave your own path.

but only because you'd rather be lonely than

lost somewhere in someone else's distinctiveness;

someone else's footprints that you'd rather not

follow.

and I see that you want to be recognized

by what you enjoy and what you desire

and the dreams you've dared to pursue.

and there is a pause in your heart when you realize

that you aren't the only one

that can take pretty pictures and inscribe potent poems

and has reveries of impacting

the lives of others.

and I know it comes in waves and it tries to convince you that you are

dispensable and forgettable and replaceable

because there are so many others

who can do what you do.

and I know you don't believe it

but none of them are you.

don't abandon that dream or that desire

or tell yourself it has already been done.

there is purpose in your passion

and a battle that has been fought, and won

so that you can know truth

and so that you can be you,

and leave a path as you go

behind you.

<u>for the sake of love.</u>

loving deeply-

past the inoperative anticipations,

and the unconcluded defenselessness.

beyond the shallow of what others see,

and into the depth of what Jesus does.

regardless of the color of skin,

regardless of religion, or culture, or political stance.

loving deeply-

into a place that has no space for

convenience, condition, or convention.

where patience flourishes,

and resentment bolts.

loving deeply,

looks a lot less like

what we tend to unveil,

and a lot more like

how He has always does.

home.

anywhere can be home,

if you stay there long enough.

beyond the comparison diversions,

and transitions,

and impediments,

lies an unblemished splendor,

in what your eyes

have not yet seen;

in what your heart

has not yet exposed.

beyond the ocean,

there are smiles waiting to acknowledge,

and arms waiting to embrace.

stories eager to be told,

and strangers longing

to become family.

home can be anywhere

you want it to be

if only you can muster up the courage,

to go, and to see.

<u>out of sight.</u>

what do you fear

the most?

a pause reverberated

as my head sunk,

an all too acquainted thought.

it sounded different coming from

his lips.

but my answer rolled off my tongue-

well-rehearsed and uncannily available-

to be forgotten I said.

to be forgotten by a person I could never

forget.

<u>looking back.</u>

but you'll always move on.

that's just how it goes.

just like your small town

home town

with broken porch swings,

and rusty stop signs,

and one traffic light.

you'll drive far enough

to have a clear view

in the rear view.

it won't be tainted with

better days

and yesterdays

that never held true.

they'll be painted with

rainbows

and tomorrows

that promise more.

after all

there's something about waking up to rain

on the pavement.

like the comprehension that the world continues spinning

even when your eyes are shut.

and it prepares a space for you-

lovely and lavished-

when the sun bursts forth in belonging.

and it reminds me how small I am.

but not in a conniving way,

more so, in a comforting one.

I can only do so much.

but nature doesn't sleep,

it's faithfulness convicts me of my own.

it doesn't move to be recognized,

or show off to mesmerize.

it won't give up, despite our

distraction clothed in our justifications and vindications.

yet there's a novelty in each morning breath

that calls for an inhale,

of pine trees and yesterday's and tomorrow's.

we might not pause to perceive it all,

but still the birds call,

and still the rain falls,

to mark a brand-new day

of promise and tenacity;

a courage for us all.

and it reminds me that I'm fallible.

but not in a way that makes me feel feeble,

rather, in a way that makes me feel fearless.

because after all, the world isn't marked by my

natal and demise.

I am nothing but a vapor in the wind,

and today I find comfort there.

it's not up to me,

there I find an exhale,

that's been calling to me for

oh, so long.

my expectations can fall,

as my relinquish stands tall.

I was never meant to do this alone.

I'm really just

so, small.

if.

my inconsistent and collapsed has always falsified

what it means to be forgiven

and to forgo what I believed I deserved and look grace

in the face and agree with that, instead.

it's hard.

because

if I'm honest,

sometimes shame fits me like a acquainted sweater

in the middle of december,

and sometimes the lyrics of the lies

are easier to retrieve.

and the truth seems too arduous

to consider and to receive.

if I'm honest,

I've always been more avoidant than avid.

and most of the time it takes all of my assembled audacity and

compiled pieces

to find the truth and pin it to my heart.

in a way that recognizes it as home

and beats to its rhythm regardless,

alone.

until it is synchronized and familiarized.

until the sunshine isn't so daunting

and the enemy isn't so taunting.

because I wouldn't believe lies, anyway.

if I could remove the disguise,

and open my eyes,

to the truth that has always wanted

to be mine,

anyway.

because of you.

and it scares me to say, but

someday, you'll be the story.

the story that readily rolls of my tongue

but not from memorization and recall,

rather speaking honest from the scars.

you'll be the story I'll tell my daughter.

when she is tangled and trembling beneath

the weight of heartbreak.

a heartbreak that's starving her

and draining her of every ounce of

vigor, and prospect, and appetite.

and she won't want to leave her bed,

she'll cry until her tears run dry

and she's left with only the scars.

I'll climb into her confusion,

and I'll lay there.

and I'll tell her of a time I felt

every bit of what she is,

now,

because of you.

<u>her.</u>

she's the glowing

in a world that's dimming.

it's shutting off the lights,

but she's just awakening her flame.

and in the chaos and clamored

I see her.

she's the smile

in a room that's docile,

the glimmer of confidence

amidst the noise and the hurt.

I see her.

her skin. her hair. her heart.

beauty beyond where

I know how to start.

I know she doesn't see it all.

comparison tears her apart.

I see her.

and it hurts me, too.

how the world can be so cruel,

and how it doesn't relent to

anyone.

I know beyond the frightened,

there's still a fight inside of her.

I can see it in the ways she speaks

and loves.

it's embodied in her embrace.

it's written all over her face.

I see her.

I wish I could whisper

it'll soon get better

because I know it will.

but I also know there's a blaze in her

that won't let her forget,

either.

I see her.

I know someday she'll see her, too.

the girl that everyone

wanted a chance to be,

including me.

she'll see the bravery that grew roots

deep down.

and her reveries that never cared to

stay put on solid ground.

and she'll see the love

that follows her around

and the flowers that have been planted

all over the ground

simply because she has lived and breathed

exquisitely.

I can't wait to see

what someday she will become

when I am beckoned and breathless

at who she is already,

right now.

I see her.

I know she doesn't see it all,

but I do.

and if you ever need to feel encouraged

that there is much life to be lived,

just see her.

mostly.

I think mostly at the stem of every tear and

heartache and insecurity and less-than,

is an intrinsic and inherent and undeniable desire

to be fully known, and fully loved.

to be known beyond the hidden and the buried,

and known beyond any attempt at distraction or depletion.

known beyond the shallow end,

and into the deep.

into the roaring waters that you sometimes need help swimming in.

known in the swiftness of the dance you fall into

when your feet forget the choreography-

the real and raw and rendering

of all of your deepest heart cries.

an echo back that says,

I see you, there, dear.

to be fully loved in the tension of every "despite."

to be loved in the fullness of fragility and fragments-

the scattered and the scorched.

loved in the middle of every mistake and circumstance

that you swore you had compiled perfectly,

this time.

to be loved like a postcard reminding you that

even the grandest of oceans cannot erase memories

and moments of together.

loved regardless.

at the core of my bravest poker face and clenched jaw and balled fist,

is a little girl who incessantly wonders,

am I truly known? am I fully loved?

and the dance continues.

for a fortified buoyancy in the depths of our souls,

that who you are is lovely and lavished upon.

and I know the same is true for you,

too.

<u>what used to be.</u>

I have nothing to hide.

I think you know that by now.

but when my honest leaves my lips,

sometimes I dread that I say too much.

I had always felt free to dance in bare feet,

beautifully in sync with the in-between.

like walking atop a fence at golden hour.

balancing boldly with both hands out,

with all of my tangled curls and a white dress

that reveled every scrape and scar on my legs,

my muddy footprints leading the way.

smiling as the sun promised me it would be back,

tomorrow.

I didn't always know caution.

it's different now.

I always make sure my shoes are tied

before I walk into a crowded room.

I always bring my armor with me.

mainly because I know that fear will meet me

in the calamity and the corners,

and it will callously chisel away at my bravery

that I tried so hard to hide in curled fists

behind my back.

until my feet start to pull me towards an exit,

and the apologies start to flow.

until I'm met with every "never mind" and

"I told ya so."

it didn't used to be this way.

I always check the mirrors before

I leave my comfort zone,

and I rehearse my lines in my head.

the lies play on repeat like lyrics of a song

I never wanted stuck in my head, anyway.

I never remember trying so hard to

match and memorize and

mesmerize with meticulous.

I had always thought dirty and disheveled

was so pretty.

I was so proud of my tattered and torn,

I thought it brought out my bravery.

I never used to plan my footing,

or only show up where I can confirm

that I'm welcome, and wanted.

it used to be different.

I used to trip over my shoelaces

and shamelessly pull my blonde strands behind my ears and

close my eyes in the face of the sun shining down on me,

reminding me that my daring and audacious

will always be good enough to greet adventure

in the face,

and conquer it all.

I used to show up with rips in my jeans and stains on my old t-shirt

and smile,

anyway.

I'm working on reclaiming my innocence

and every ounce of shamelessness.

I'm working on it.

I haven't forgotten what fearless feels like.

<u>closing time.</u>

you receive me like an old friend-

a friend I never remember inviting over.

one I don't particularly miss, either.

and you've only destroyed

every notion of who I thought I was.

you've relentlessly chased me down,

only to steal my crown

and throw it on the ground,

and remind me of all that I'll never be.

you'll reveal to me all of their best,

and dangle it alongside each of my less-thans,

and remind me of every crack and crevasse

that causes me to stumble and shutter.

but I have to tell you,

I'm learning to love my chipped and chiseled.

envy isn't enticing, anymore.

I don't wish and wonder about who I could be.

I actually bask in contentment and delight in who I am already-

who I've been molded and mended into.

I've learned that appreciation and recognition of all of my best

and my worst has carried me

here.

right here.

and I know that I don't need to be anywhere except

right here.

how beautiful for me, right?

and how dreadful for you.

because I refuse to allow space in my corner for you anymore.

your voice has been revealed and exposed

in my heart as the venom that it has always been.

I don't know how this all began,

but I'm cutting all ties.

there's nothing here to mend.

farewell,

comparison.

you are not my friend.

<u>a commission.</u>

be the one.

the foretaste of light amidst the disarray and demanded.

like the signaling of a door ajar after countless closed.

like a brave little aspen tree in the middle of autumn

colorful and thriving amongst all that is dying.

be the truth in a world of trickery and tidy.

as steadfast as the serenity of the sunset,

and as sure as the sunrise to precede it.

be the one that chooses uncovered innocence,

the one to welcome others to dance in that, too.

the one who speaks up when others shutter and stare.

the one who protects like a promise

and defends through every "despite."

the one who grabs hands and guides home.

be that one.

the world needs more of you.

about the author

jessie is a 23 year old colorado native and is a poet and a writer. this is her first poetry book, and plans to continue to write and publish more in the future. she is passionate about honesty, authenticity, and the pursuit of passion, which shines through in each of her poems. she is also a well-known faith and poetry blogger, and you can find her on Instagram as @wildflowerwritings. jessie is always looking to connect and engage with her followers- just shoot her a message!

facebook: wildflower writings
instagram: @wildflowerwritings
blog: wildflowerwritings.weebly.com

Made in the USA
Middletown, DE
14 November 2018